W9-CIM-620

# happy anniversary

# happy anniversary

words of love for couples to share

edited by jo ryan

Published in the United States in 2008
by Tangent Publications
an imprint of
Axis Publishing Limited
8c Accommodation Road
London NW11 8ED
www.axispublishing.co.uk

Creative Director: Siân Keogh
Editorial Director: Bili Edwards
Designer: Sean Keogh
Production Manager: Jo Ryan



ISBN 978-1-904707-66-0

9 8 7 6 5 4 3 2 1

Printed and bound in China

# about this book

A beautifully designed collection of thoughts and sayings, *Happy Anniversary* is an ideal gift for partners, lovers, and couples on their anniversary. The words of wisdom and inspiration express the joy, happiness, and humor of falling in love, being in love, and staying in love. It is a book to treasure, to dip into for inspiration when life is getting you down.

Complemented by evocative, cute, and tender animal photographs, *Happy Anniversary* is a celebration of the excitement of love and partnerships.

# about the author

Jo Ryan is an editor and author who has been involved in publishing books and magazines across a wide variety of subjects for many years. From the many hundreds of contributions that were sent to her, from people from all walks of life and all ages, she has compiled a collection that celebrates love, relationships and marriage.

Love is what makes
two people sit in
the middle of a
bench when there
is plenty of room
at both ends.

Friendship
doubles our joy
and divides
our grief.

Meeting you was fate,
becoming your friend
was a choice, but falling
in love with you I had
no control over.

There is no feeling more
comforting and consoling
than knowing you
are right next to the
one you love.

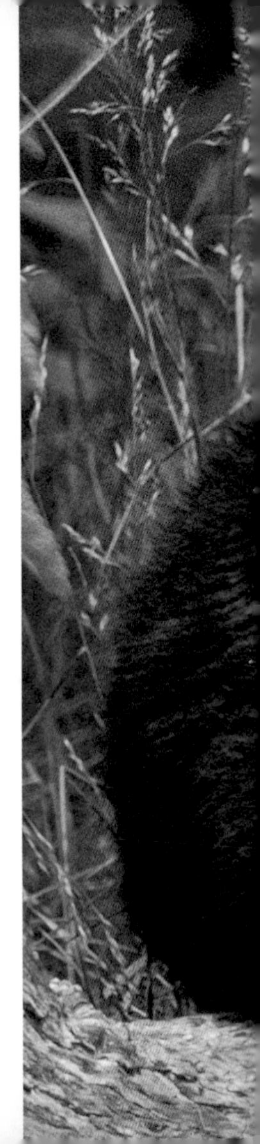

"I love you not because of who you are, but because of who I am when I am with you."

Love is the thing that
enables a woman to sing
while she mops up the
floor after her husband
has walked across it in
his barn boots.

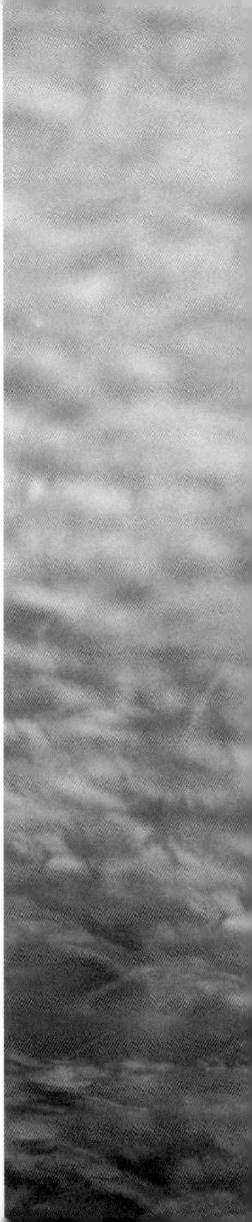

“No man is worth your tears,
but once you find one that is,
he won't make you cry”

Never go to bed mad.
Stay up and fight.

Love is not singular
except in syllable.

Are we not like
two volumes
of one book?

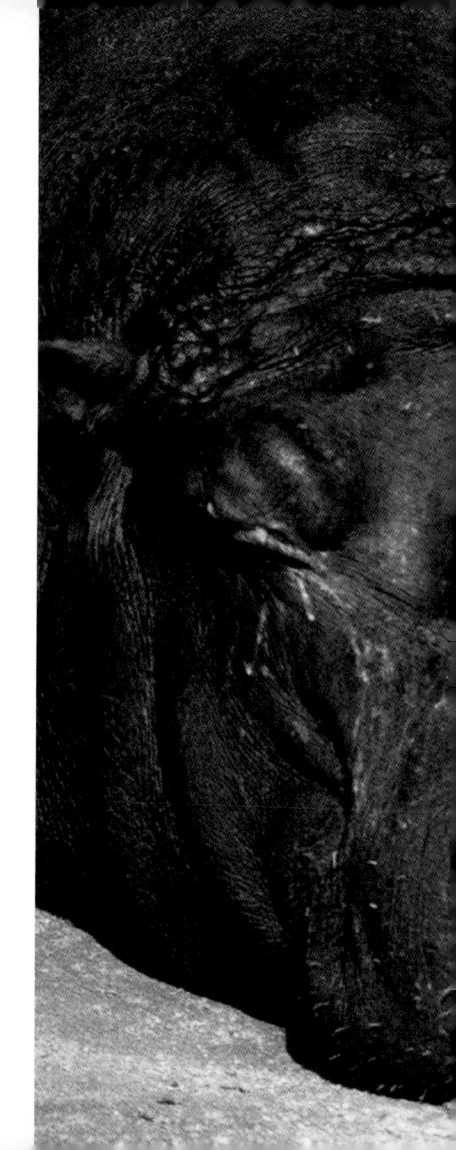

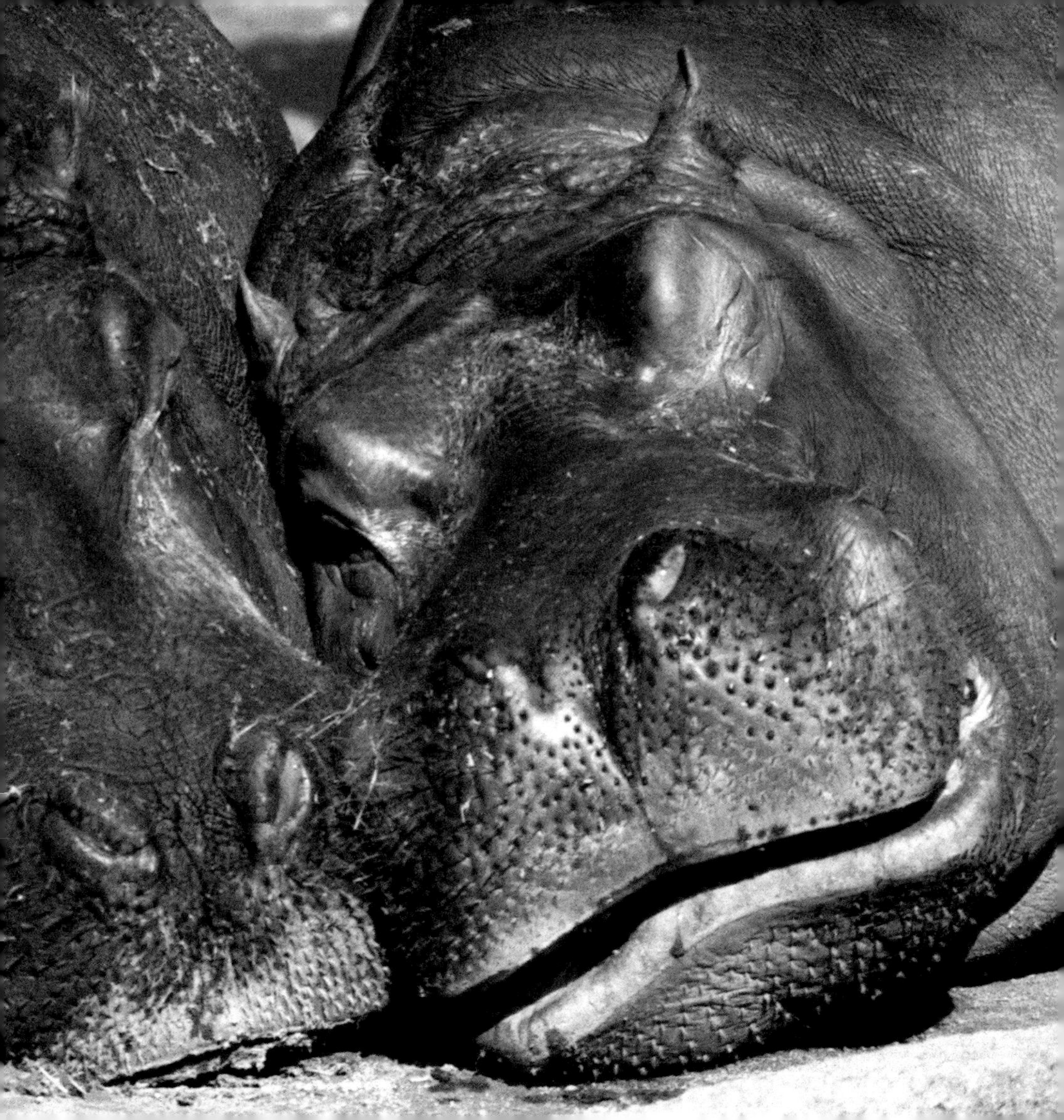

A good wife always
forgives her husband
when she's wrong.

A successful marriage requires falling in love many times, always with the same person.

The difficulty with marriage is that we fall in love with a personality, but must live with a character.

The bonds of matrimony are like any other bonds—they mature slowly.

A wedding anniversary is
the celebration of love, trust,
partnership, tolerance and
tenacity. The order varies
for any given year.

Our wedding was
many years ago.
The celebration
continues to this day.

Spouse: someone
who'll stand by you
through all the trouble
you wouldn't have had
if you'd stayed single.

An anniversary is a time
to celebrate the joys of today,
the memories of yesterday,
and the hopes of tomorrow.

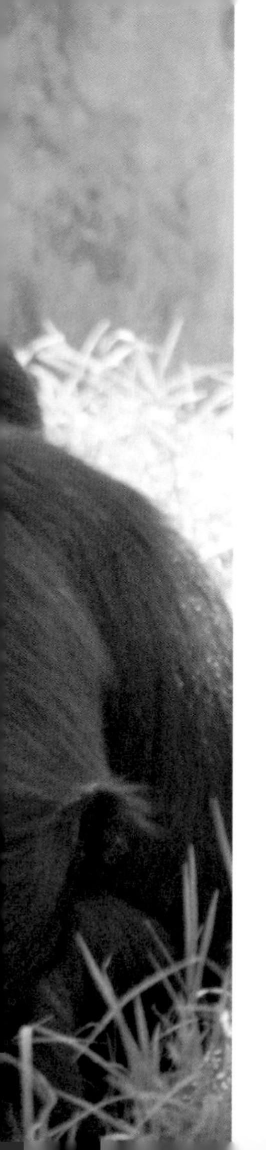

The highest happiness
on earth is marriage.

A happy marriage is a long conversation that always seems too short.

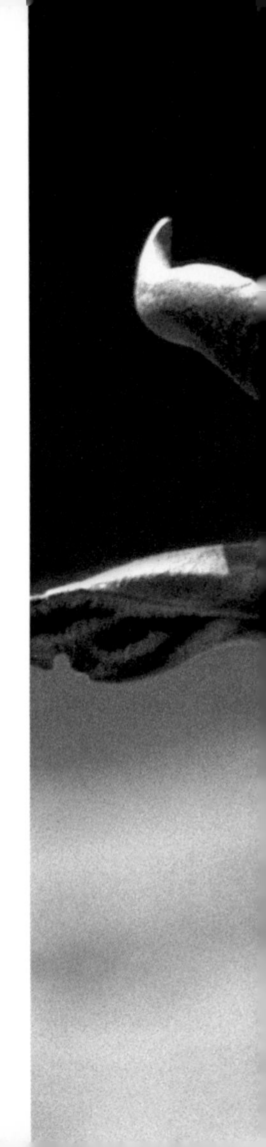

If I never met you,
I wouldn't like you.
If I didn't like you,
I wouldn't love you.
If I didn't love you,
I wouldn't miss you.
But I did, I do, and I will.

Love me when
I least deserve it,
because that's
when I really
need it.

It's so great to find that one special person you want to annoy for the rest of your life.

Love one another and you will be happy. It's as simple and as difficult as that.

Lust dies...

True love lasts forever.

Love as if you've
never been hurt.

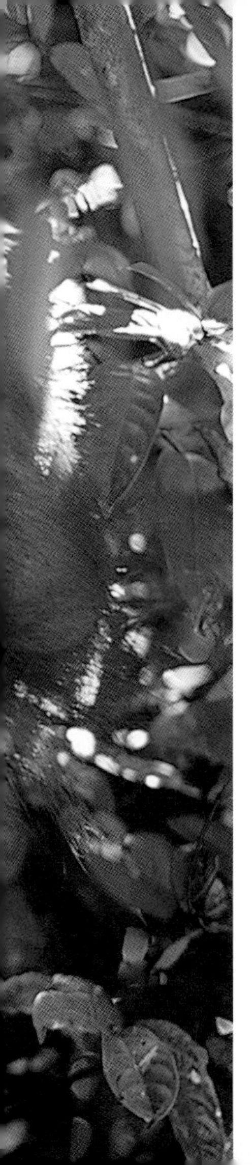

Life without love is like...
body without soul.

If you judge people to quickly, you don't have time to love them.

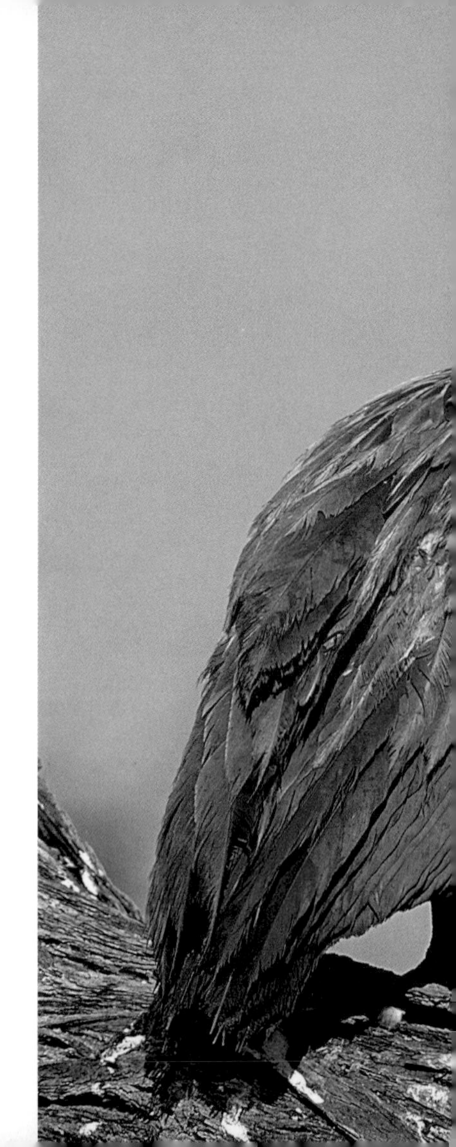

Love everyone more
than yourself, especially
those who love you
more than the world.

True it is that
marriages be
made in heaven
and performed
on earth.

To the world you're
just one person,
to one person you
are the world.

I could search my
whole life through
and through and
never find another you.

Do you believe in
love at first sight?
Or should I walk
past again?

Love isn't what makes
the world turn, it makes
the ride all worthwhile.

Love does not consist
of gazing at one another,
but of looking together
in the same direction.

You don’t love a woman
because she is beautiful,
she is beautiful because
you love her.

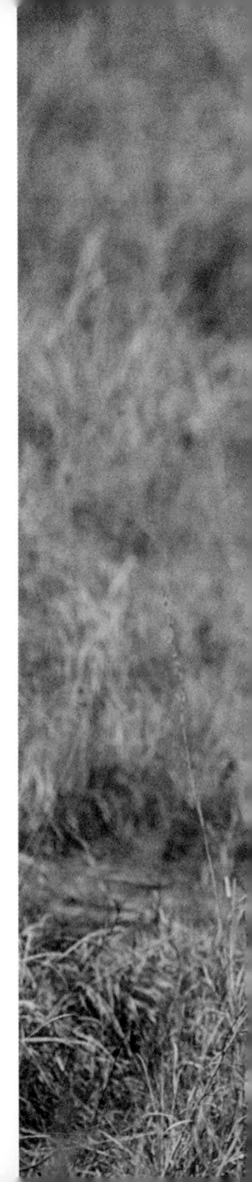

Love brought you together
as husband and wife,
and gave each of you
a best friend for life.

A life without
love is like a year
without summer.

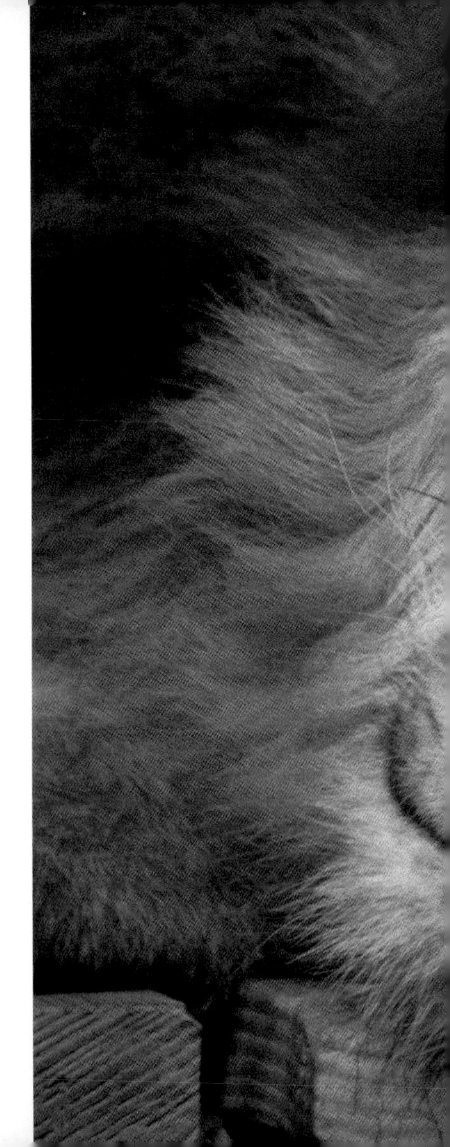

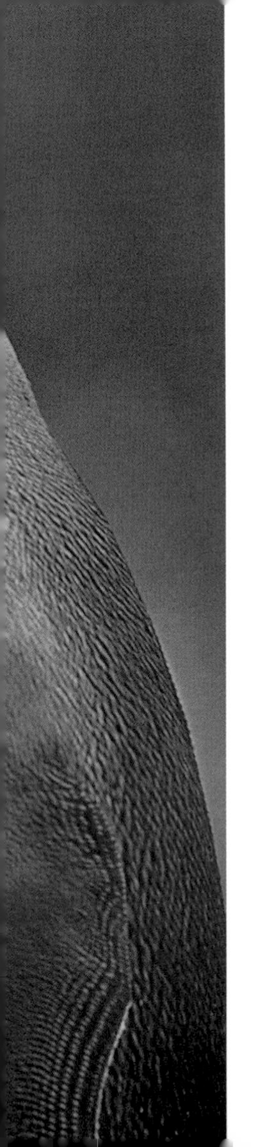

Love is just a word until
someone comes along
and gives it meaning.

If I know what love is,
it is because of you.

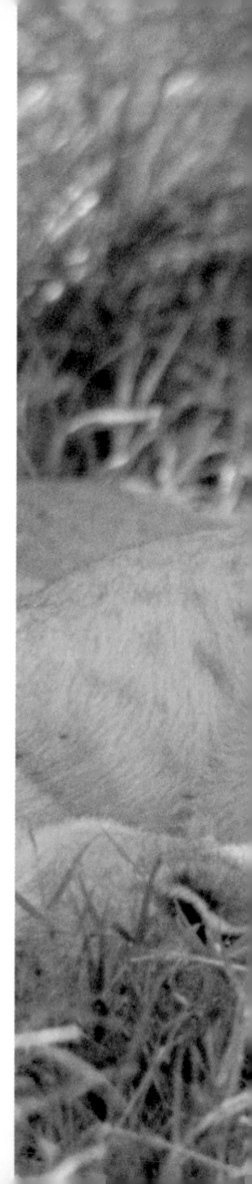

Married couples who love each other tell each other a thousand things without talking.

Love is the greatest refreshment in life.

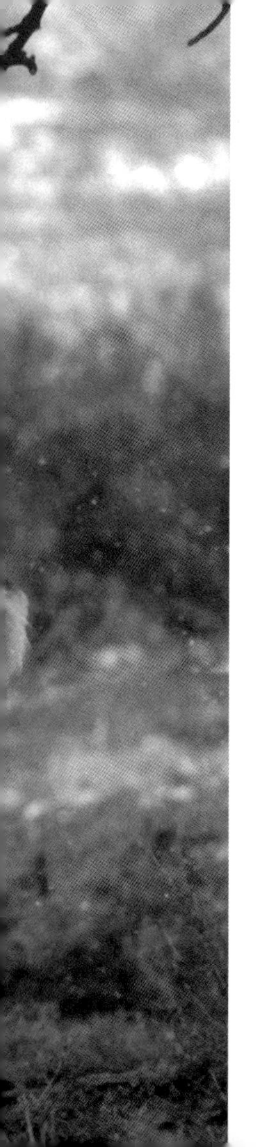

You don't marry someone
you can live with—you
marry the person who you
cannot live without.

We are a work in progress with a lifetime contract.

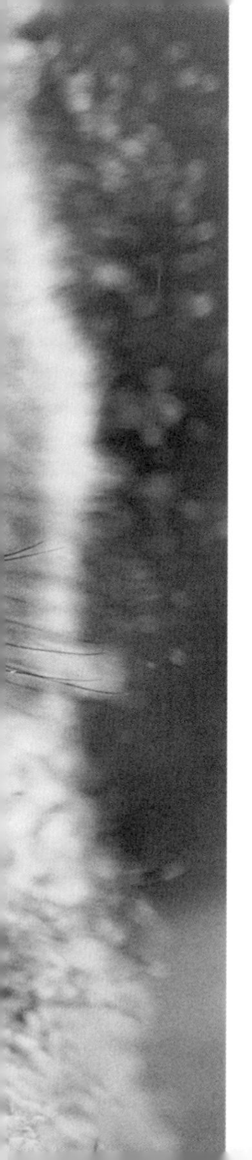

Marriage has many pains, but celibacy has no pleasures.

Love is composed of a single soul inhabiting two bodies.

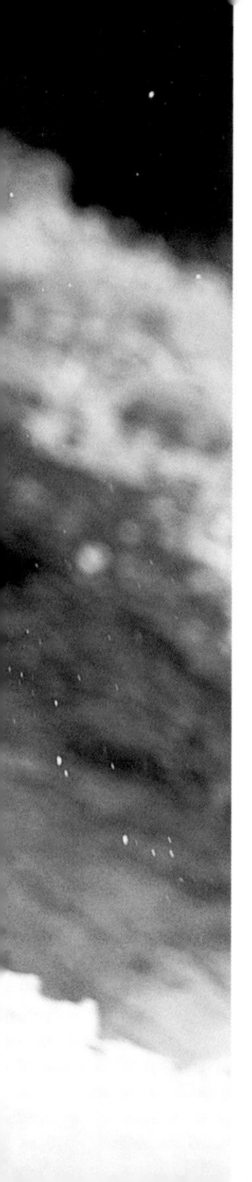

When you meet someone
who can cook and do
housework—don't
hesitate a minute—
marry him.

Marriage is our last, best chance to grow up.

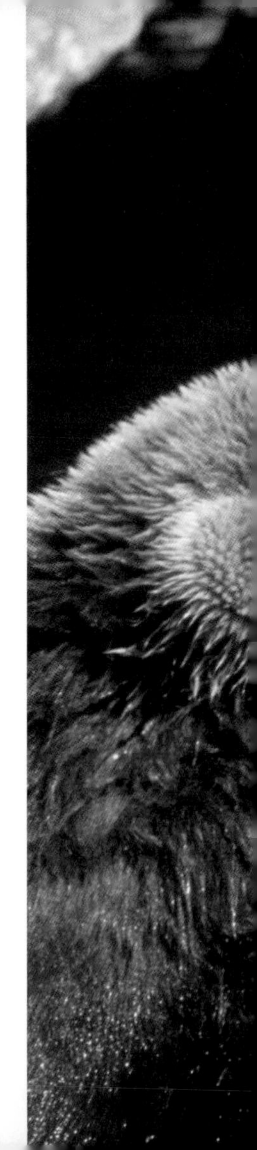

To love someone deeply gives you strength. Being loved by someone deeply gives you courage.

Remember that happiness is a way of travel, not a destination.

There is nothing nobler or
more admirable than when two
people who see eye to eye keep
house as man and wife,
confounding their enemies and
delighting their friends.

What lies in our
power to do, lies in
our power not to do.

Men are from earth.
Women are from earth.
Deal with it.

Let the wife make the husband glad to come home, and let him make her sorry to see him leave.

In all of the wedding cake,
hope is the sweetest of plums.

A good marriage is
that in which each
appoints the other
guardian of his solitude.

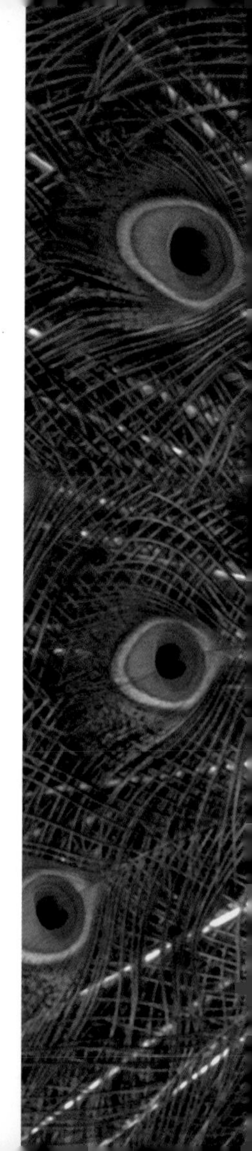

You know you're in love
when you can't fall asleep
because reality is finally
better than your dreams.

Love is the condition in
which the happiness of
another person is
essential to your own.

The world has grown suspicious
of anything that looks like
a happily married life.

True love never has an ending.